Poetry from the Heart

Poetry from the Heart

To Julie.
Thankyou for your support.
Best Wishes for the future.
  Love
  Karen Hiett

Karen Hiett

To order additional copies of this book, contact:
Xlibris Corporation
0-800-644-6988
www.xlibrispublishing.co.uk
orders@xlibrispublishing.co.uk
501152

Contents

This book is dedicated to my wonderful husband Gary and my two sons Leslie and Jessie. I love you more than words can say. Thank you for your love and support over the years. You are all truly amazing.

Introduction

I started writing poems in 1983 when my Nana died. The words seemed to flow from pen to paper without me realising what I was doing. Over the years I have written poems to family, friends and work colleagues for special occasions or events in their lives. The people I have written a poem for all have a special place in my heart. I find it hard to show my feelings face to face and express myself and poetry is the best way I have found to say what I truly feel.

We have become involved in a children's home in Malindi, Kenya called God Our Father Home for Needy Children. We are constantly trying to fund raise for the orphanage to try to make life easier for the staff and the children. Every year we visit and see a vast improvement in the accommodation, grounds and equipment, which makes us more, determined to continue helping. All profits from this book will go the God Our Father Home for Needy Children to continue to try and make a small difference to their lives. My work colleagues help me to raise the money, we have bake off's selling cakes and other food; some people will just give us a donation. I will be forever grateful to them for their time, support and hard work. All ingredients are donated so every penny goes to children. I have added some photos of the children throughout the book so you can see how beautiful and well looked after they are. They are very happy and special each and every one of them. Mama Susan is an incredible lady that works tirelessly for the children as well as looking after her own family and we feel privileged to know her.

I would like to take this opportunity to thank you for purchasing this book and helping to support the children's home and hope you enjoy reading my poetry.

Karen

God our Father home for needy children

It was about 6 years ago we went to Kenya as it was my dream,
Little did I know how tough life could seem.
We passed an orphanage on a day trip one day,
Arranged to pop in and hoped it would not dismay.
We got out of our car stood in disbelief,
The children looked so happy what a relief.
We were shown around by Mama Susan who is in charge,
This woman was amazing and her heart so large.
She cared so deeply for every child that was there,
How could we walk away after 1 visit and not really care.
We gave them some things that we took over on the plane,
Never realising we would be so affected and never feel the same.
The children's faces glowed with such hope,
My heart ached and very nearly broke.
We looked at each other straight in the eye,
Pledged that we would try to continue to help we said with sigh.
We returned home and went back to work,
The pain in my heart went from an ache to a hurt.
Told my stories to friends that would listen,
A seed planted and we started to see the vision.
If we could help in a small way,
We could brighten up the children's day.
Every year we return to see the children and have some fun.
Enjoy these wonderful people making the most of lives in the sun.

04-10-2010

Leaving

The time has come at long last.
Enjoy yourself, have a blast.
7 years of toil, hard work and stress,
Now have a break and enjoy the rest.

I have enjoyed the laughs and the chats,
Gossiping about the work place rats.
I wish you well and may all your dreams come true,
Hope your mornings will stop feeling so blue.

For Clunie

24-02-2010

Elvis

I have been waiting 33 years for this day,
To stand at your grave and have my say.
I always adored you and loved your voice.
Would loved to have seen you live, I would have rejoiced.
My heart broke that fateful day,
When you were so cruelly taken away.
I remember so fondly watching you on a show,
The smile on my face would lovingly grow.
Thank you for all you have achieved and done.
For making Rock and Roll history and giving us so much fun.

For Elvis Presley

April 2010

Smells

Rumour has it there is a nuclear attack,
Oh no it's Adeola making a snack.
As we sit here smelling your dinner,
This smells like a loser not a winner.
We all sit holding our noses wishing the stink to go,
Open the windows, fresh air will flow.
Vegetables are good for you they say,
Maybe you should try a bale of hay.
A threat of incense is a compromise you offer,
Another stinky smell, oh bother.
We love your sense of humour and fun,
But your smells make us want to run.

For Adeola

10-06-2010

The card

I thought of you when I saw this card,
Tried to walk past it but it was too hard.
I picked it up and memories became clear,
Thought of you having a beer.
I had to buy it and put it in the post,
Our childhood memories I would like to toast.
There is no occasion to send this card,
Except walking past it was just too hard.

For Craig

14-06-2010

Diet Blues

As I approach the station I hear a rumble,
Is that my train or my stomach I mumble,
Should I stop and grab something to munch,
Or should I be good and wait for lunch.
One day I will be a size 14,
Ain't been that size since I was a teen.
Will power is what I need to find,
Poxy diet is a bind.
I walk into my office, try to hide my aching hunger,
Rumble, rumble my stomach sounds like thunder.
Oh my life I need something to eat,
A big bar of chocolate would be a treat.
Waiting for lunch time to come around.
I look in my drawer and drool at what I have found.
I try to hide it so I am not tempted,
My snack box has now been emptied.
My belly if full, now I feel a naughty girl.
Poxy diet is living hell.

For Adeola

13-08-2010

Congratulations

Now we can celebrate at long last,
Your fear and pain no longer need to mask.
Meeting your new son you have longed for,
Show him your love, hide the pain that has been so raw.
You will make wonderful parents of that I know,
Hold his hand, watch him grow.
We are so proud of your commitment and your strength,
Always here for you, will go to any length.
Support you may need to begin,
If that's the case give us a ring.

For Mo and Chris

Moving on

Gladioli are tall, colourful delicate flowers,
Adeola is a manager that does not cower.
She stands full of Caribbean grace,
Wants us to take part in a charity race.
She enjoys having fun but can be firm,
Upset her and you may feel your fingers burn.
She asks for loyalty and respect from her team,
Give it to her then she won't be so mean.
It has been fun having you here for this short time,
I now feel at ease and can say you are a friend of mine.
Our sense of humour tends to run in parallel lines,
Lots of laughs we have had many times.
You have given me some precious memories to keep,
Like cracking up on the kitchen floor in a heap.

For Adoela

01-09-2010

I Wonder

I wonder what would have happened if Jessie had been born alive,
Or if you had not been the twin to survive.
Wonder what would have happened if you had been given that
   gun,
For that we have to thank your Mom.
Wonder what would have happened if your family had not been so
   poor,
Would you have listened to the Blues through that open door.
Wonder what would have happened if you had a different boss,
Would we have known you, that would have been a terrible loss.
Wonder what would have happened if you had not gone in the
   Army,
If they hadn't given you those pills to keep you awake, stop you
   going barmy.
Wonder what would have happened if your Mom have lived to be
   an old lady,
Would you have married Priscilla and had your beautiful baby.
Wonder what would have happened if you'd had more control,
Would you still be here to Rock and Roll.
Wonder what would have happened if someone had told you No,
Would you still be here to perform live in show.
I have spent years wondering what if and why,
Why you took drugs to make you high.
You was a precious gift and you are loved by so many,
You left us with a hole in our hearts that is so empty.
Your memory and songs are here forever,
We will never forget you Elvis, especially in black leather.

For Elvis Presley
Written on 10-08-2010

Happy birthday

Happy birthday to someone who is so dear,
You are so special I tell you, don't you hear.
I know things have not gone to plan,
Thankfully you don't need to rely on a man.

I am only just a phone call away,
There to speak to any time of day.
You hold a special place in my heart,
Only miles keep us apart.

Cheer up my very special friend,
I always have an ear to lend.
Show the world your wonderful smile,
Light up the world mile by mile.

For Lee-Lee

17-02-2009

The official OAP

To the apprentice lolly pop man
Hold this sign in your hand if you can.
Watch the ankle biters cross the road,
Teach them to remember the green cross code.

All old men have a job to fulfil,
You might need help, so pop a pill.
Don't hit them on the head with your sign
Or you might end up doing time.

For Ken

March 2009

Friendship

A friend is someone who will never let you down,
A friend is you that I am so glad I found.
I am always here for whenever you need me,
You hold the gift of friendship, yes you hold that key.

I feel I have know you for many years.
Sat, held hands and shared many tears.
You make my world so complete and sincere.
Fill my life with lots of hope and cheer.

Your friendship is so special to me.
I hope you share that too, I hope you see.
I hold my hand out to you for you to take.
This friendship is true and not a fake.

Thank you for being there for me.

For Mo.

Food

Got a full belly I heard you say,
I had a very good lunch today.
Waddling around trying to strut my stuff,
Staying close to the toilet, feeling a bit rough.
What's that over there in that dish,
Oh chocolate cake, please find some room I quietly wish.
Just a little piece to take to my room,
Hope my belly don't go boom.
Need a drink to wash it down,
Well it is lunch you say with a frown.

For Adeola

03-08-2010

Keep safe

I have an Angel deep in my heart,
I want to share it with you, to help you depart.
She will help to protect you while you are away,
And bring you back to us safe on another day.

This Angel is in words and you cannot see her face,
Her powers are impeccable; she will always be on your case.
Carry her with you wherever you go,
Protection and love from her will glow.

Be safe, happy and take lots of care,
Have fun Hun and do not despair.
We will be waiting for you to come back home,
You will have plenty of love around you wherever you roam.

For Imelda

06-07-2010

Re-hydration

One cup, two, cup another cup three,
Oh my Lord I need a wee.
Re-hydration will keep me well,
Shame the toilets look like hell.
They bring me water all day long,
Well I am the manager is that so wrong?
One cup, Two cup, three cup, four,
I will finish this poem before it becomes a bore.

For Adeola

12-08-2010

Retirement

I know we have had our ups and downs,
Sometimes our sorrows we could have drowned.
Had loads of laughs and moments of despair,
Family worries we would compare.

May your retirement be totally stress free,
Put your feet up with a big hot mug of tea.
I hope that any disputes have been laid to rest,
I would like to take this moment to wish you all the best.

Keep safe.
For Ufi

Birthday wishes

It is your birthday, so cheers to you,
Here are some words for you to digest and chew.
You have changed so much in the last year,
Happier and settled I have noticed with cheer.
You have so much to look forward to and to plan,
Building a new life with your family and clan.
It is a pleasure getting to know the new you,
Watching you change and seeing life in a new view.
I wish you all the very best on this special day,
I like to say I am proud of you if I may.

For Allison

30-06-2010

Your last day is here

So this is it, your last day is here.
If we drank we would have a beer.
We have known each other for many a year,
It feels like you have always been here.

We have had some chats in the fag room,
Tried to avoid chats of doom and gloom.
I value your friendship and the time we have had,
I know you are glad you are retiring but I am sad.

The memories I have of you will stay deep in my heart,
I know, I know you are calling me a silly old fart.
But how can I let you leave without saying how I feel,
My love and friendship for you are real.

I look forward to hearing all your plans and news,
How lovely your new life is, and not hearing your blues.
Make the most of everything that comes your way,
I will shut up now, I have had my say.

For Val

09-07-2010

Recovery

One snip here, one snip there,
National health service really do care.
Give it a week or two and you will feel better,
Might even feel obliged to write a thank you letter.
Put your feet up and be nursed by Mo and Ross,
Let your work place feel the loss.
You will soon be back having a game of golf, with the boys.
Typical geezer back playing with his toys.
We wish you a speedy recovery real fast,
And look forward to having a good old laugh.

For Chris

30-09-2010

Wedding Day

Although you have lived together for years,
Being married truly endears.
It unites you both forever as one,
Enjoy the day and have loads of fun.

Wearing a wedding band on your finger,
Stops you feeling so singular.
Marriage makes you feel so special,
But can help you to feel more mental.

Standing together showing the world your love,
Surrounded by invisible white doves.
I give you both my love and best wishes
And blow you both loads of kisses.

For Alison and Peter

August 2009.

Rover

You deserve the very best,
Probably more than all the rest.
Now the wait is almost over,
What's his name? Is it Rover.

When he is happy he wags his tail,
Just be careful, mind your mail.
Give him lots of love and kisses too,
Maybe give him something good to chew.

He will bring you lots of joy,
You will say "What a good boy"
He will be your hearts desire,
When he lays on your feet by the fire.

1995

Football Mad

I like football very much,
Except when the ball hits my crutch.
Sometimes I play when it's very cold,
Covered in grass, I look like mould.

I like football it's a good game,
Bobby Moore should be my name,
My favourite bit is scoring a goal,
Must remember not to hit the mole.

I like football wet and muddy,
Even better when it gets bloody.
When I get home I have a hot bath,
Then remember the game and have a good laugh.

For Jess

What to do

Leslie, Leslie what will I do,
All I do is worry about you.
I seem to be trying so hard,
It is making me feel very tired.

We want you to change your school,
Then maybe everything will be cool.
We want lots of things for you,
Why don't you tell us what to do.

Just want to make everything right,
Then we will not to have to fight.
You are a very special boy,
How can we help to make you life a joy.

For Leslie

Another year

Another year has passed,
Didn't it go by so fast.
Driving around in that company car,
Didn't get you very far.

We think you are great,
Even when you are sometimes late.
You are always on our minds,
Well ok, just sometimes.

We will miss you when you go,
You must pop in and say hallo.
This is all we can think to say,
We will end this poem if we may.

Memories

I will always remember special times,
With you beside me, mountains I could climb.
Remember you standing in your Judo kit,
Sitting proud, amazed and amused I would sit.
Wanting to be as good as you,
I learnt some of your skills too.

Proud that you are my Dad,
For life, not just a fad.
Always there through thick and thin,
Could take the knocks of life on your chin.
Words of wisdom still ring in my ear,
They still make me think when I fear.

Leslie and Jessie idolize you too,
Enjoy watching the things that you do.
An example they are proud to follow,
There that's our Poppa what a fellow.
Someone to look up to and admire,
As long as you are around, they will aspire.

Life seems so very short looking back,
Even though we have taken lots of flak.
Memories are special and I see them clear,
The price we pay for them is not so dear.
Thank you for everything you have done,
Now I face the world and no longer run.

For Ron Hawes (Dad)

20-06-1999

A brother is

A brother is someone to admire,
To be like him is your desire.
Well respected by his kin,
Always wanting to know where he's been.

A brother is someone you always trust,
Learn from his lessons is a must.
Love him with all your heart,
Hope you will never part.

A brother is your best friend,
Even if he drives you round the bend
Always they're to lend you a hand.
Isn't life with him is just grand.

My brother is you Larry,
The Father of our little Harry.
I am so very proud to say your name,
Life without you would never be the same.

For Laurence

24-08-2000

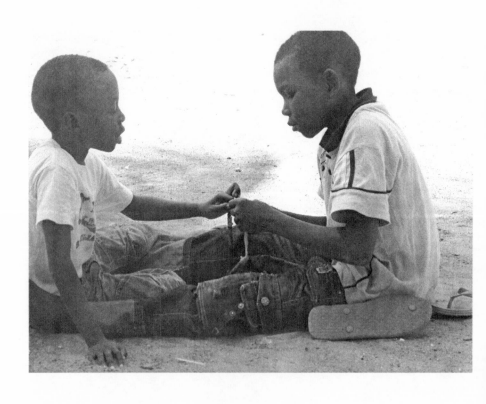

I believe

I believe Angels are our guides,
They help us silently and stay by our sides.
Angels are our loved ones that have moved to a better plain,
They guide us through tough times and whisper our name.
Our family on the other side are our Angels,
They help us when our lives are in shambles.
Keep your Angels safe and remember they are there,
Because our Angels are the ones that really care.

For Debbie and Jodie

30-09-2010

New home

So you have grown up and have your own home,
No longer a child finding a playground to roam.
Independence, housework and bills,
Put the heating on to stop the chills.
I am so happy that Ben and yourself have settled down,
Cuddle up close, you can loose that frown.
I love you so much my wonderful Louise,
When I see you I will give you a huge big squeeze.

For Louise

28-10-2010

Sisters

I can't believe I have known you for 40 years,
In that time we have both shed a lot of tears.
Friends and foe we have been in the past,
As sisters we have shown our love will last.

From Daddy's girl to my best friend,
Always there with a hand to lend.
Life has not been easy for either of us,
We try to cope without too much fuss.

We left school with our dreams in our hearts,
This is where the adult stuff really starts.
We both went on our separate ways,
Marriage and children took up the days.

Our parents are the keys to our lives,
Through them our love survives.
Dinner every Wednesday night, cooked by Mum,
Tears of laughter during dinner. Oh what fun.

Now you are 40 years old,
As tales of our youth unfold.
Memories last forever in your heart,
May all our memories live forever and never depart.

For Lynn my Sister

July 2001

Special moments

I have seen you grow from baby to lady,
Heard progress reports almost daily.
You are very special to those who care,
Give them your hand for help if you dare.

I see your face it's imprinted on my heart,
Sometimes think you silly tart.
I smile when I think of you, enjoy the hugs we share,
Special moments sometimes seem so rare.

I know deep inside you have the strength to win,
This journey will be hard but to win is not a sin.
We need you to be strong and well,
We know you can get through this hell.

We are always just a phone call away.
Look forward to hearing from you any day.

For Louise

Mum's the word

After you pushed me into the world,
In your warm, loving arms I curled.
Safe, secure and wanted I felt,
What a good hand of cards I was dealt.

Years passed by, I began to find my feet,
Lots of family and friends I would meet.
There you stood with that smile on your face,
With you by my side I could win this race.

I left school and began to earn a crust,
Your love for me I would always trust.
Strength and compassion you gave to me,
My destiny soon became plain to see.

Leslie was born he struggled at first,
Love and attention he would thirst.
Nanny was a blessing and someone to trust,
Love and cuddles from you he would lust.

Jessie came into the world later on,
Again your love was still very strong.
Both boys adore you, as you are so sincere,
You hold they key to our hearts that's so clear.

This is a chance to try and say what I feel,
Words are so hard to say, In writing it states what is real.
Thank you so much for everything that you have done,
Life with you has been such wonderful fun.

For Mum on Mothers day.

22-03-1998

Watch out Haley's about

Another woman driver on the road,
You say "I'll have that car". "ok it's sold".
L plates torn up in half,
I'll go for a spin after my bath.

Independence at long last,
I'd better not drive too fast,
My tank is full and I am raring to go,
Why is this Muppet driving so slow,

Elliot is waiting by the shop,
I hope there is somewhere for me to stop.
Hurry up and get in, I'm on a yellow line,
Do you like my new car, it's all mine.

How about a cuddle in the back,
Can't be long or I will get the sack.
It's now time to got back home,
I want to give my Mum a phone.

For Haley

12-07-2001

An ode to Princess Diana

There you stood shy and coy,
The good old days full of joy.
Then came the surprise of your life,
When Prince Charles asked you to be his wife.
You gave him the Heir of the throne,
You wrapped up Wills and took him home.

As time went by you became so strong,
Just like us you sometimes did things wrong.
Everyone began to love your smiling face,
Then the press and public began the rat race.
Freedom was a word that became a dream,
Sometimes you would fight to get away from the team.

Your sons were the light and meaning to life,
After a while you were no longer a wife.
You held your head high and struggled on,
But regardless to everything you still shone.
The Nations adored all your hard work,
Then life is gone in one unfortunate quirk.

You will never be forgotten.

For Princess Diana

August 1997.

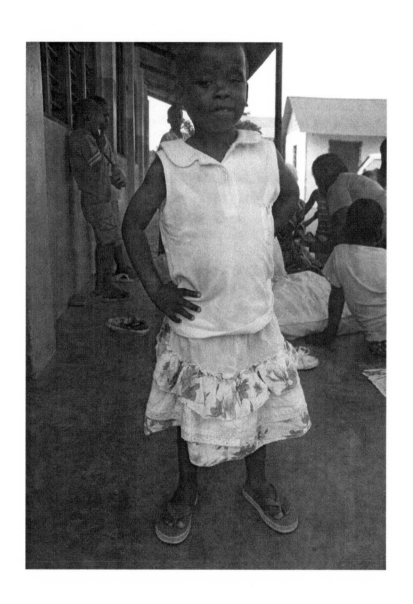

A new life

Hoping your future is all you desire,
All your dreams completed before you retire.
Someone as special as you are,
Will always twinkle like a star.

Your kindness and love you fondly share,
A quality that now seems so rare.
Memories of you will stay in my heart,
The magic moments will never part.

Follow that road that destiny gave,
Love, luck and fortune you will have.
Take my love and wishes too,
This little ditty is especially for you.

For Sandra

November 1997

Good news

1998 already seems a good year,
Good news I heard from two people I hold so dear.
Feelings tell me that this news is so right,
Remember this when you hold each other tight.

You both deserve love and luck to come your way,
I wish to congratulate both of you if I may.
You are very special people who should have the very best,
Hope your lives are full of love, laughter, cuddles and zest.

For Sandra and Brian

January 1998

A tribute to you

Life here won't be the same,
Everyone involved in this horrible game,
We will miss your helpful ways,
How will we cope with the future days.

I feel sure that things will work out right,
Although we fought with all our might.
We did unfortunately lose this war,
But fate has opened a new door.

With your family and friends you will reign,
From that strength you will gain.
Here's wishing you all the very best,
Hope you new job is full of zest.

For Jan

December 1997

A retirement ditty

Wishing you well as you retire today,
All your dreams shall come your way.
Take it easy, have lots of fun,
Put your feet up and lie in the sun.
Enjoy your new life with family and friends,
With love and wishes this ditty sends.

For Trish

August 1997

A new horizon

So the rumours are true,
A new job is in line for you.
Life here has been so trying,
You can breath without sighing.

How will we cope once you have gone?
Life here is the same old song.
They think admin is a doddle,
Maybe they will hire Glen Hoddle.

Hope you achieve the respect you deserve,
You will do well, you have the nerve.
Contentment I am sure you will feel,
Good wishes I send, that's for real.

For Fran

20-03-1998

Loves special gift

As you hold Andreas in your arms,
You will notice his special charms.
Love and security he will thirst,
Even when he is at his worst.

Endless demands it will seem,
Worth it though, you'll know what I mean.
A child is the most valuable gift,
When you are down he will give you that lift.

Father and son are a man's dream,
Mother and son make a wonderful team.
Here's wishing all three of you all the best,
Good luck, congratulations and all the rest.

For Irene

03-07-1998

Destiny Shines

Although life sometimes seems so hard,
Suddenly someone throws you a good card.
Take it in your hand and hold it tight,
At the end of the tunnel shines a wonderful light.

You both have someone to love and treasure,
The sun will shine no matter what the weather.
Hand in hand you'll be shown destiny's path,
Enjoy the ride and keep making loved ones laugh.

In your hearts you both hold the key to love,
Over your heads shall fly beautiful white doves.
Peace is here, feel the calm.
Love has become your special charm.

For Sandra and Brian

27-06-1998

Reunited

I feel we have always been together,
In Scotland we will inhale the heather.
I will wear your ring with pride,
Feel secure with you by my side.

To be your wife again is all I desire,
Being together until after we retire.
Together we shall see life through,
Because you love me and I love you.

Leslie and Jessie are doing well,
It has been tough, sometimes almost hell.
We will always have our memories in our hearts,
Hearing their laughter on the go-carts.

Grand parents is going to be our next role,
Don't look so scared you poor old soul.
Babysitting will be such fun,
Playing with the grand children in the sun.

As we age the boys will look after us,
Remember not to make a fuss.
I love you more than words can say,
You are my sunshine, you make my day.

For Gary (my husband)

Kyra Jayne

"Push" they said
Hurry up I want to go to bed.
"When will our baby be born"
You said with a very big yawn.

"Here is the head"
Les rushes down the bed.
"I can see it crowning" he said with glee,
"Oi what about about looking after me"

"It's a girl" I heard then cry,
"Thank God that's over I thought I would die"
Kyra Jayne was born on the 10th May
Isn't she beautiful I heard you say.

"How do you feel Sue? Now that is all over",
"Relieved thanks, bring that cup of tea over".
Daddy is looking after the baby,
Hopefully he will carry on when we get home, well maybe.

Devon loves his little sister,
When he leaves the hospital he said "I will miss her"
Kyra has so much love to give,
We will feel it for as long as we live.

Kyra you are such a special girl,
More valuable than the most expensive pearl.
Hope all your dreams come your way,
The 10th of May will always be such a special day.

For Kyra, Sue and Les

08-06-2001

My love

As I look at your face,
My heart begins to race.
To see you smile,
Beats everything else by a mile.

As I look into your eyes,
You make me feel the highs.
To hear you laugh and see you play,
Makes me feel lucky. You make my day.

As I hold you in my arms,
I feel safe and feel your charms.
To love you as much as I do,
Always stops me feeling blue.

As I feel your body against mine,
Makes me want you for the rest of time.
To wipe away any fears,
You stop me crying tears.

As I realize how special you are,
You are my life, my lucky star.
Thank you for being there,
Without you life I could not bear.

For Gary (my husband)

A gift of love

Waiting for the day to come,
Feels an eternity for some.
Then all of a sudden the day arrives,
It always comes as a surprise.

"Harry is here", you say with such pride,
"Hush my darling" soothing him as he cries.
Comfort and warmth Harry will bring,
Will make you feel like Queen and King.

Such happiness and joy will come your way,
Watching him grow is great, I will hear you say.
Introducing Harry to his two big brothers,
Together they will get into all sorts of bothers.

With you both beside him he will learn,
Giving you lots of love in return,
You both made this precious gift,
He will give your life such a lift.

For Laurence and Pauline.

12-07-1999

An ode to Colin

There was a man called Colin West,
He always tried to change things for the best.
Unfortunately he sometimes made things worse,
We are beginning to think he is a curse.

All his workmates stood by him,
Said "Things can't be that grim"
Just persevere and it will work out,
We just can't suss it out.

We all try different ways,
On and on for days and days.
In the end it will be ok,
As long as we all shut up and obey.

For Colin

Grandchildren

First a girl then a boy,
Your heart is again filled with joy.
Spoil them rotten, then send them home,
Hear them gurgle on the phone,
Being a Nan is so much fun.
Always on your toes, always on the run.

Having Grandchildren is our hearts desire,
Gives us an excuse when we retire.
"I am a Nan" we say with so much pride,
Hugging them tightly when they cried.
Make the most of it and enjoy the fun,
Shut up Dad, remember you are my son.

Snuggled up cute as can be,
Come here darling and sit on my knee.
Nearly time for you to go home,
Get your coat, let's give you hair a comb.
You can visit me whenever you like,
Next time you can bring your bike.

For Jackie

19-11-2001

Jade

You made us laugh, you made us cry,
Now you are a star in the sky.
You always shone so bright,
We will always see you at night.

No words can say how we feel,
Especially when we heard you was ill.
Your strength and humour made us proud,
Made us smile when you laughed out loud.

You're a legend and will always be in our hearts,
Even though we lived worlds apart.
Keep your boys safe and sound,
Because we know you will always be around.

For Jade Goody

16-03-2009

Wish you well

I am sorry you are not feeling well,
Hope you ain't going through too much hell.
Being waited on hand and foot,
Wishing you was the one to cook.

The doctor has given you some pills,
Thankfully you don't live in USA and have huge bills.
I am sure you will soon be back up on your feet,
Running the house like a copper on her beat.

For Helen

03-06-2009

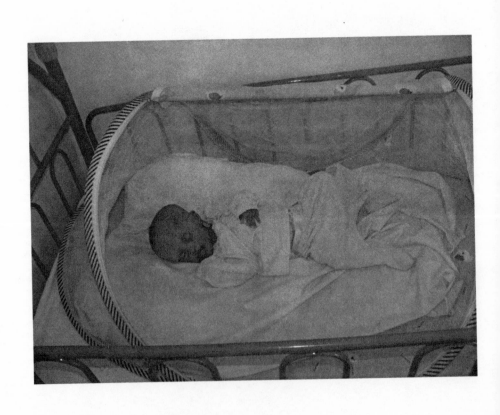

Duty

Being on duty is such a laugh,
Telephone queries, oh what a blast.
Answering calls all day long,
Think we deserve a bloody gong.

Sitting here typing up all the notes,
Not much time to tell some jokes.
Oh here we go, that phone is ringing again,
They cut of, that's a shame. Amen.

Hoping for time to eat my lunch,
What happens, calls come in a bunch.
Trying to speak with my mouth full,
Hoping for a temporary lull.

Time is going pretty quick,
Dam the ink has run dry in my Bic.
Only half an hour to go,
Then I can hit the shops and spend my dough.

Best wishes

Hustle and bustle has been your life,
Always making sure everyone else is alright.
The time has come for you to let go,
Relax a little become more mellow.

You have been a gift to those you love,
I would like to thank our friends up above.
I feel honoured and lucky to know you,
Your friendship has been nothing but true.

Spoil the cats, shop with QVC,
Go to the beach and paddle in the sea.
Have a lay in and enjoy the rest,
Here's wishing you all the very best.

For Jacqui

The cackle

Her laugh has been describe as a cackle,
Which is an improvement to the death rattle.
Her humour is sometimes close to the edge,
Almost makes me fell like jumping off the ledge.
The building comes alive when we hear that cackle,
And we are so happy it isn't the death rattle.

Written for Cindy

04-10-2010

A token

A small token for you Debbie dear,
From an orphanage in Malindi, their struggle so clear.
Your support and kindness means so much,
May it bring you good wishes and luck.
The children are so special and make us smile,
For them we will walk that extra mile.

For Debbie

09-2010

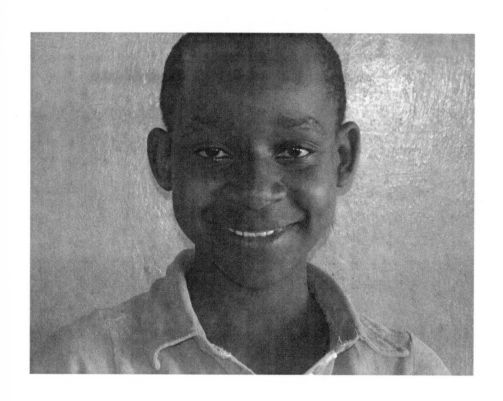

Baking skills

This is for you to say thank you Gill,
We had 2 weeks in bliss without a chill.
It was made at an orphanage near where we stayed,
Not a machine in sight and all hand made.
Your baking skills helped in our dream,
To try to bring some comfort and stop life being so mean.

For Gill

09-2010

For you

Allison this is a thank you to you,
From an orphanage we found out of the blue.
The children are so tender and mild,
You feel what love can come from a child.
Your commitment and friendship means so much to us,
Your honesty we will always trust.

For Allison

09-2010.

Appreciation

A small thank you to you dear Ann
Taken to an orphanage nearby in a van.
This bracelet was made by the children all by hand,
Doesn't it look special and so grand.
The children are a joy and fun to be with,
Makes us appreciate the lives we live.

For Ann

09-2010

From Malindi

This is a thank you just for you Cindy.
It was made by the children from an orphanage in Malindi,
Their smiles so heart warming they make you melt,
Even with the rough cards they have been dealt.
We can't solve all the problems that are here,
But your time and effort we hold so dear.

For Cindy

09-2010.

Special thanks

This is a thank you to you dear Shangle,
The price for this we did not wrangle.
It was made by an orphanage near where we stayed,
We stopped for a while and were shown what they made.
You helped us raise a substantial sum,
May all your dreams truly come.

For Shangle

09-2010.

My Brother

I have a brother that I love called Ron,
If he were Italian he would be the Don.
Surviving by ducking and diving,
But one of his loves is fast cars and driving.

Brought up his daughter virtually alone,
No one can say he has a heart of stone.
Kerry Jane has grown onto a beautiful Mother,
She is happy and content, that's all down to my brother.

He is a granddad with so much life,
And he does have a very caring wife.
Always up to his neck in water and muck,
He is clever and can work his way out of a ruck.

He is always there for his family and friends,
Very good at fixing, building and even his tools he lends.
I love my brother with all my heart,
Even when he is being a silly old fart.

For Ron

21-10-2010.

Ice Queen of Wickford

I hear you have been watching dancing on ice.
Don't try to copy them, please take my advice.
Slipping and sliding all over the place,
Another emergency, another hospital case.
Up to your neck in a plaster cast,
Enjoying the attention, cards, presents what a blast.
Alfi and Daisy will want to write on your leg,
Best you keep it hidden and stay in bed.
We wish you well and get better soon,
And stop being a total loon.

For Charlotte

03-02-2010

A message

Nana and Poppa are now together,
Their love will now last forever.
They now leave us all behind,
With many pictures in our minds
Our love for them will always last.

For eternity they will not be parted,
Their love has always lasted.
Together they stand together holding hands,
Our love for them as always stands.

Heaven is a place for those who die,
In paradise they both do lie.
Resting now in eternal peace,
Our love for them will never cease.

For Jessie Burr (my Nana)

Dec-1983

GOD OUR FATHER
CENTRE FOR NEEDY
CHILDREN HOME
P.O BOX 1664
MALINDI
26/9/2010

Dear Community care Advice center
Hello how are you I hope that you are all fine and doing well. We
are also fine and doing well. The main reason of writting this
letter is to say thank you for what you did for us. Thank you
for the money which you send. Every body in God our path
is happy and singing Jambo mbwana. May God bless the
work by your hands thank you so much. We all love you.
We would also wish to see you

BYE BYE SO much

Thank you

MAY GOD BLESS U ALL

kwaheri!!
kwaheri!!
BYE BYE

From Samuel Shukran

We Love You

God Our Father Centre
For Needy Children
PO Box 1664 - 80200
Malindi - Kenya

Dear Community Care Advice Center.
Hello! How are you? I hope you a fine
I am fine too. My name is Precious Zawadi
Karana from God Our father.
The main purpose of writing this letter is just
to tell you thank you for everything you
have offered to us. Thank very much for
your love and may God bless you very
much.
We Love you and we will
be remembering you everyday.

GOD BLESS YOU

WELCOME TO GOD OUR FATHER

GOD OUR FATHER

I ❤ YOU

WELCOME AGAIN
TO God Our
Father.

FROM
PRECIOUS ZAWA

GOD OUR FATHER
FOR NEEDY CHILDRENS
HOME

DEAR

COMMUNITY CARE ADVICE CENTER

HELLO

HOW are you, I hopping thats your are
fine In the Name Of Christ
Iam writing this Latter for what you
have done for us and Iam Saying
THANK your for buying for us School Shouse
School uniform and Slipers and Iam
Saying My GOD BLess you for Jobs you
have done for us
Iam Saying to Get More thing than that

MY GOD BLESS YOU
So MuCH
THANKS

We Love
you

ERICK   ERICK STEVEN

DEAR Community Care Advice Center.

Hello! How are you I hope you are fine, I am fine too. The cause of writing this latter I just to say thankyou for what you done for us. lets God bless you so much even the work of your hands lets God bless it.

We realy love you so much and we are praying for you everynow and then. Thank you so much for surpoting us and remembering us you just continou surpoting us and remembering us and God will bless you whatever you do. And where you go God we be with you and where we be no way God with you give you a way. My name is Gladys I am in Std Seven and I am doing well in my School. And I wish to go to class eight next next year. I love you somuch may God bless you.

I LOVE YOU SOMUCH

FROM LOICE.

GOD OUR FATHER,
CENTER FOR NEEDY,
CHILDRENS' HOME.
P.O. Box 1664 - 80200,
MALINDI - KENYA.

Dear Community Care Advice Center

Hello! How are you? I hope you are fine I am fine too. My names are Loice patience Mtuku I am 13 yrs old I live in God Our Father Childrens Home. The main thing of writin this letter to you is just to thank you for your support. you've ~~let~~ Supported us very much. We also thank you for things you send for us and for the money that you ~~send~~ Send for us. Thank you for sending Caren and Gary they did a shopping for us and they bought alot of things we can't count them. We all say thankyou so much and may God bless you and the work of your hands. We love you all. Bye! Bye

I ♡ U   THANK YOU so much.   I ♡ U

GOD BLESS YOU.

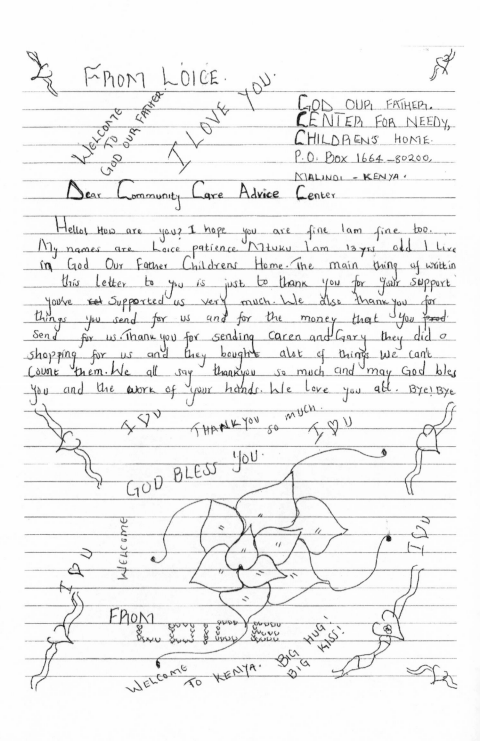

Welcome

I ♡ U

I ♡ U

FROM LOICE

WELCOME TO KENYA. BIG HUG! BIG KISS!

GOD OUR FATHER CHILDR
HOME P O BOX 1664-
80200 MALINDI
KENYA - WATAMU

Dear Community care Advice Centre

How are you I hope that you are fine
and doing well. I am fine and doing well here in
God our father Children's home in kenya.
The aim of writing to you this
is to pass may regards and you also allow me to
this golden wonderful Chance to thankyou for
your Support and love that you have shown
to us and the Money that you sent to
us and everything that you have bought to u
we are so much greatful and may the
Almighty God bless the work of your hand
Thankyou very much we love you
so much thankyou for being concerned of
God our father Children's Home

yours lovely boy

BYE

Fred

I ♡ U All

MAY God BLESS YOU

SO MUCH

Lightning Source UK Ltd.
Milton Keynes UK
04 January 2011

165172UK00001B/104/P